Heligan Centenary Guide Book

including Four Tours of The Gardens and Estate and a Brief History of their Creation

Written by Candy Smit
Text © Heligan Gardens Ltd.

Cover photo courtesy of Sylvia Davies

All sepia photos © Tremayne Family Archive and colour photos © Heligan Gardens Ltd. (photographers include R. Stafford, L. Tremayne, J. Stephens, C. Smit, L. Curry, R. Perkins, C. Harvey, G. Hunt, C. Stobart) unless otherwise stated

All maps updated by Russell May
Hand-written chart by Ruth Perkins

Booklet designed and printed by St. Austell Printing Company
on FSC Cyclus Offset 100% recycled paper.

Published by Heligan Gardens Ltd; 2014
to mark the Centenary of World War 1
ISBN: 978-1-900270-03-8

Updated 2016 & 2017

The Lost Gardens of Heligan are open daily all year round from 10am
except for Christmas Day

For further information telephone 01726 845100
or contact us at:
The Lost Gardens of Heligan,
Pentewan, St. Austell, Cornwall PL26 6EN

www.heligan.com
www.facebook.com/thelostgardens
www.twitter.com/heligangardens

Introduction to our Living Memorial

Welcome to Heligan during 2014-18, as we mark the centenary of World War 1. During this period a hundred years ago Heligan Gardens changed dramatically from a vibrant Edwardian Garden at the peak of its development, both technically and horticulturally, to a shadow of its former glory; tended by a third of its workforce for essential duties only... and increasingly peopled by ghosts.

Between 1860 and 1901, Squire John Tremayne and his wife, the Hon. Mrs Mary Charlotte Tremayne (daughter of 2nd Baron Vivian of Glyn), had supervised developments in the grounds of Heligan personally – as keen, skilled and eventually renowned gardeners. They supported a sizeable indoor and outdoor staff as well as a family of three daughters and a younger son, John Claude Lewis (Jack) Tremayne, who inherited not only Heligan but also a number of other properties in Cornwall and Devon upon his father's death at the start of the 20th century.

Squire Jack Tremayne (born 1869), a gentleman with no family of his own, ran a somewhat reduced household and transformed his predecessors' interior from heavy Victorian to relatively minimalist, stylish Edwardian. The family album illustrates these changes to his home as well as the transition to horticultural artistry within areas that had necessarily been more strictly productive during his father's era.

The Heligan Estate Workbooks of 1914-17

These evocative books record staff names and daily outdoor jobs, including wages. In August 1914 there were 23 on the pay roll, with names filling each page top to bottom; by 1917 there were only eight. Over this period the steadily increasing lines left blank on each page speak louder than any words... However, as we mark the centenary of World War 1 on site, it is not our intention to replicate this historic loss of labour, nor the resulting decline of the gardens.
Photo © Charles Francis, courtesy of North Devon Record Office

The entrance hall at Heligan House in 1908

Jack did not continue the family tradition of going to Oxford. After spending time in Rome with his uncle, Sir Hussey Vivian (the British Ambassador), he joined The Duke of Cornwall's Light Infantry in 1894 and became a Captain in The 3rd Battalion. By the outbreak of World War 1 he was too old to go to the front, but he served as Asst. Director of National Service for the West London & District Area.

Only a month before war was declared, Jack had given another family property, Croan near Wadebridge, to his only married sister, Grace Damaris Babington, for her 50th birthday. Her five sons were subsequently to serve in the Army, Navy and Royal Flying Corps; two lost their lives during this period and the others earned very substantial honours - Jack's eventual heir (one of these nephews), Sir John Tremayne (*né* Babington), being awarded both the DSO and Legion d'honneur for his outstanding wartime service.

Jack Tremayne was one of the first landowners outside London to offer his property for use as a convalescent hospital for wounded officers of the Royal Flying Corps. His personal circumstances determined this significant gesture and he is known to have given his own time here. In recent years, archive from this period has arrived in our hands in plenty; whatever the past trauma, his home clearly provided a haven and an opportunity for less complicated recovery, in dream-like surroundings. Heligan certainly played its role in the healing process a century ago.

It is not, however, this Tremayne family link with World War 1 that has given the modern-day Lost Gardens of Heligan their critical association with the period. It is the fact that the garden restoration itself, which took place during the 1990s, was specifically undertaken in the name of Jack Tremayne's outdoor staff, many of whom gave their lives in service on the terrifying fronts across the channel.

Tim Smit's introduction to Heligan in February 1990 was through John Willis, the contemporary representative of the Tremayne family who had just taken responsibility for significant parts of the Tremayne Estate. Only weeks after the Great Storm at the start of that year, the two of them were macheteing through fallen giants on an initially casual mission to investigate John's inheritance.

This, however, was to become a seminal moment in Tim's life, for during that single visit he became hooked on the mysteries of this place and committed himself to find out what had happened here. He returned immediately with his builder friend, John Nelson, and within days of discovery The Lost Gardens were being explored (almost daily) by the two of them, like some unheard-of foreign land. Even on their first foray together, each one knew that their lives had changed forever as they gave their hearts to Heligan.

Tim and John Nelson's critical moment of discovery was within the devastated Melon Yard, which revealed two ruined cubicles of gardeners' toilets – one of which, on excavation, still displayed the pencil signatures of past staff. This early Victorian Thunderbox Room had attracted graffiti over many years; but Tim recalls the faint date 'August 1914' below a column of names and this soon inspired fruitful local research.

Today this 'Thunderbox Room' has become, in the term spontaneously awarded to it by the Imperial War Museum in 2013, a 'Living Memorial'. Though their signatures have now faded, the sacrifices of 'The Gardeners of Heligan House' have been recorded in the museum's new, online, UK National Inventory of War Memorials, specifically compiled to mark the centenary of World War 1. (Visit www.ukniwm.org.uk and search for entry 63622.) This is an honour indeed that was not sought, but earned by the men who worked the soil here a century ago. (Some of their stories are recounted in tragic detail in our separate booklet, *Heligan History Centenary Edition: Remembering Lost Men.*)

Another generation has grown up since the restoration of The Lost Gardens began. There is a constant cycle of review and renewal, with big projects still ahead. Our whole outdoor team is deepening its commitment to investigate past practice and to extend it beyond the gardens and out into the wider bounds of the Heligan Estate as well. Our desire is to honour the past, enrich the present and demonstrate a course for the future.

Convalescent officers beside the Celtic Cross outside Heligan House
Photo courtesy of Penny Russell-Grant

A Brief History of The Gardens

Heligan House a century ago, with C18th stable block and clock tower visible, on the left

Heligan has been in Tremayne ownership for over four centuries. An earlier house was purchased by Sampson Tremayne in 1569. Participation in the English Civil War for the Royalists then prompted a decline in family fortunes over several generations; but one John Tremayne was appointed a Knight of the Realm by King William and Queen Mary in 1689 and he subsequently funded significant stylish developments to the house – which included a first gesture to the formal gardening style of the period. In 1735, his great nephew, also John Tremayne, on his marriage to Grace Hawkins, commenced a number of projects which gave substance to the house and immediate surroundings, including a parterre garden to the front and a new stable block and clock house to the rear. However, it was their youngest son, Henry Hawkins Tremayne, who was to take the first steps towards the framework of The Gardens and Estate that we recognise today. He was the first of four successive squires who were responsible for the lay-out and historic plant palette that remain.

Henry Hawkins Tremayne (1741-1829)

Although trained for a career in the Church, Henry Hawkins inherited Heligan in 1766 at the age of 24, when his remaining older brother died unexpectedly. During his lengthy tenure he increased the family fortunes through marriage and quite distant inheritances, accumulating estates in North Cornwall and in West Devon as well as significant mining interests through his father-in-law, John Hearle of Penryn. He was a man of sufficient substance, action and good reputation to leave a lasting mark on the landscape of Heligan.

In early 1774, Henry's resident younger sister Grace recorded in her diary the regular visits of a Mr. Hole, whom we know to have been the surveyor and draftsman of the first known – and still awesome – 1777 Plan of the Heligan Estate. This showed the structural features that existed; Heligan House still in William and Mary form, the farm buildings, Heligan Mill and the ancient tracks that connected everything to the world beyond – with neighbouring landholdings labelled.

A journal dated 1785 describes in detail a journey Henry later took by coach and horses, around southern England (and up as far as Birmingham). His purpose was to educate himself in current landscape fashions, particularly inspired by Gilpin and Shenstone. Numerous visits are recorded in ecstatic detail... to Blenheim Deer Park, Park Place at Henley, Stowe, The Leasowes and Hagley Park near Halesowen, Piercefield near Chepstow and Hestercombe in Somerset... to list just the recorded highlights!

This early sight-seeing tour clearly inspired Henry to commission plans for the romanticising of his own estate, whose network of natural watercourses and steep interconnecting valleys offered an ideal backdrop for landscape embellishment. Thos. Gray's 'Plan of Intended Alterations' (undated, but certainly pre-1810 – before the house was re-designed in Georgian style) illustrates a substantial proposal to open up the views from Heligan House and to create a sweeping new drive direct to the front door, through fashionable shrubberies. Tree-lined carriage drives were marked, offering

Miniature of Henry Hawkins Tremayne by William Bone R.A., 1795
Photo © Charles Francis

routes through the old woods, and later maps suggest a small 'temple' was actually built at the very highest point immediately to the south of the estate. Gray's plan includes the suggestion to incorporate a field which matches the footprint of the present gardens, as part of the new designed landscape. The curve of the beautiful back wall of the Melon Yard is shown too. These incredible early masterpieces are all held by the Cornwall Record Office – format does not allow reproduction here.

It appears that during Henry's tenure, the Georgian Ride through what we now call Lost Valley was set out and embellished with specimen trees and the Eastern Ride in today's gardens was created, leading up to the position of the Northern Summerhouse, taking in a superb coastal view. The same small Flemish bricks were used for the temple mentioned as well as for the Northern Summerhouse and the large walled garden that we call the Flower Garden; all are dated to the very early nineteenth century.

From within the Northern Summerhouse, restored with original cobbled floor

Henry's wife, Harriet Hearle, died in 1813, leaving Henry ageing alone for a further 16 years. Archived correspondence from his only son, John Hearle, suggests that they communicated by post, frequently daily, and shared the interests of family, staff and estate, native plant propagation, health of livestock and diverse issues of contemporary existence, including developments in mining, agriculture and domestic politics, as well as events abroad.

John Hearle Tremayne (1780-1851)

On his father's death in 1829, John Hearle inherited a substantial and promising portfolio! Born in 1780 and married in 1813, his early adult life pivoted around three centres: London, where he served between 1806 and 1826 as one of only two M.P.s representing Cornwall (and where all bar one of his eight children were born); Sydenham House near Lifton in Devon, a convenient half-way house offering respite – particularly for his wife and poorly eldest son; and Heligan, his eventual prime 'seat'. His wife, Caroline Matilda Lemon, was one of the numerous daughters of his fellow M.P. for Cornwall, Sir William Lemon. Though John Hearle is reputed to have been more interested in his farm and his woods, it was through his wealthy in-laws based at Carclew near Falmouth that he secured for Heligan the early horticultural prestige of being the first place in England to successfully propagate the unusual *Cornus capitata* from Nepal. After an initial national announcement in a beautifully illustrated article in the 1832 *Botanical Register*, it was John Hearle's gardener, J. Roberts, who was specifically credited for the achievement, in the 1834 edition of *The Floricultural Cabinet and Florist's Magazine*. (He did not stay long in the squire's employ!) Also, through John Hearle's brother-in-law, (Sir William's

only surviving son) Charles Lemon, who sponsored Joseph Hooker's expedition to Sikkim (1848-51), Heligan later acquired material from the renowned Hooker Collection of rhododendrons – some of which survives in the gardens to this day.

Photo © D. Hastilow

Cornus capitata,
first known as Benthamia fragifera

The 1839 Tithe Map of the Parish of St. Ewe shows in detail the structures and productive grounds at Heligan, which included by this time the Melon Yard and Kitchen Garden. These supported a vibrant social life at Heligan House, particularly as John Hearle and Caroline's offspring became of marriageable age! Rides down through the woods on horseback or by carriage along the new Georgian Ride were frequently recorded by a visiting diarist, Barclay Fox.

John Tremayne (1825-1901)

John's passion for horticulture took Heligan Gardens to the peak of its reputation during his fifty-year tenure as squire. He had a serious interest in the developing science of hybridisation and was keen to follow contemporary trends, particularly the acquisition of newly imported exotic plants, including Orchids. Veitch's Nurseries (in Exeter and London) and later Treseders in Truro would have been prime suppliers, though John Tremayne and indeed his son Jack travelled to the continent themselves, to collect seeds and purchase camellias and exotics.

The shape of the Flower Garden has been trapezoid from its incarnation, to maximise the use of the sun, but associated structures and walled enclosures went through several configurations during the nineteenth and early twentieth centuries, with the Paxton House appearing in the 1860s. The remaining structures on the north side of its supporting wall are an essay in Victorian horticultural heating technologies, with survivors from various phases of development. The productive gardens of Heligan would have reached a peak in the fine-tuning of crop production, including the forcing, retarding and storage of fruit, vegetables, flowers and herbs. The first of the Heligan Ram Pumps was installed down in a steep valley on the, then, western edge of the estate, representing the start of a shift from reliance on well water.

Where the development of the pleasure grounds is concerned, John Tremayne enhanced his grandfather's shrubberies with an extensive collection of Camellias and Rhododendrons as well as other new and interesting ornamental trees; he supported his wife in the creation of the Sun-Dial Garden and his son in the development of what we now call The Jungle. In April 1891 there was a big freeze which would have wiped out most of the tender collections down there. Hence much of what you see in this extraordinary exotic valley today dates from the very end of the nineteenth century.

John Tremayne captured by Bluck of London in 1874, an image circulated on his election as M.P. for East Cornwall
Photo © Charles Francis

Jack Tremayne (1869-1949)

The last resident squire of Heligan played a major role in the development of the gardens from an early age, encouraged by his parents. He had artistic flair and a great enthusiasm to experiment with the wealth of new plants that were being imported to these shores for onward sale – sourced by this time not only from North and South America but also Asia and the Antipodes.

Jack also supervised the updating of horticultural technologies, adding to the estate infrastructure another Ram Pump, the large Reservoir on the northern edge of the gardens and the Britannia Boiler in the Head Gardener's Office. It is unclear when the Peach House would have been added to the glasshouse collection in the Flower Garden. It first appears on a map published in 1907, though the glazing style dates back to the 1880s. This 1907 OS map was then used for a land valuation four years later, which hand-records, as a recent addition, a free-standing glasshouse whose overgrown ruins were discovered in 1990 – and which we may still seek to restore.

Bearing in mind most of the visitor routes today were old paths excavated and re-instated by volunteers during the early 1990s, we are using the 1907 OS map in this guide as a reference for your own exploration today. The achievement of the recent garden restoration is evidenced by how little has altered from a century ago... and so, we are now pleased to accompany you around Heligan – as though Squire Jack Tremayne were your host and the grounds had just reached their first maturity.

Squire Jack Tremayne driven by his chauffeur (possibly Mr. Harry Cullum) in his 06-1905 Charron-Girardot-Voight 25CV side entrance tourer!

Tour Options

The grounds open to the public today necessarily encircle Heligan House (now sold off as flats) at a respectful distance; but they have nonetheless been restored to original purpose – with productive gardens 'feeding the household' and training staff while the pleasure grounds create a stunning venue for relaxation and 'occasional hospitality to the community'! There are almost 200 acres accessible to our visitors, as there would have been nearly 200 years ago. Something for everybody... You are most welcome.

Our Entrance facilities are close to The Gardens, the prime focus of the Tremayne's horticulture passions and our recent restoration. They encompass around 37 acres; with productive areas strung down through the middle like a beating heart, flanked by Eastern and Western Rides which link a diverse collection of concealed individual gardens and features of the period. The ground slopes slightly to the south and the paths are mostly of gravel.

Beyond The Gardens, the pastures of the Heligan Estate stretch away to the east and to the south, cross-cut by several steep valleys that eventually lead down to Mevagissey; one of which contains our fabulous Jungle garden.

We offer you a choice of four themed tours. They knit fairly seamlessly together for a grand day out, or you can select T1 or T2 (or both) on less challenging terrain for a more leisurely stroll – though there are several access issues for wheelchair users on T2.

A map showing these two Garden Tours marked in colour is on the front flap of this booklet. Inside this front flap, two Estate Tours (T3 and T4) are also shown in colour, on a wider area map. The following pages of tour descriptions are colour-coded to match.

Use your separate, larger Free Map for more specific contemporary visitor information and if you are a wheelchair-user, please check also for details on our Wheelchair Access Map. Beware! Tour 4, particularly, covers extensive challenging terrain.

Exotics line the back entrance

T1 – Main Garden Features:
Start at Ticket Office and follow signs to The Gardens: Flora's Green, Kitchen Garden / Melon Yard / Bee Boles / Flower Garden (incl. glasshouses and working buildings), Sundial and Scented Gardens / Sikkim, Italian Garden / Western Ride / The Ravine – EXIT AND REFRESHMENTS, TOILETS, INFORMATION etc.

Heligan House garden party in 1908 (courtesy of Frank Grigg)

T2 – *Curiosities*:
Start at the Ticket Office and follow signs to The Gardens: Left up Western Ride / Beacon Path / The Mount / Northern Summerhouse, Eastern Ride / New Zealand / The Grotto, Reserve Yards / Wishing Well / Heligan Sawmill and Workshop – STEWARD'S HOUSE CAFÉ (Toilets, Picnic and Play Area). Return via The Gardens or onward via East and West Lawns / Woodland Walk (Woodland Sculptures and Giant's Adventure Trail) – EXIT etc.

T3 – *Animals*:
Start and end at the Steward's House: Home Farm & Wildlife Hide

T4 – *Explore: Woodland Sculptures, Lost Valley and our fabulous outdoor Jungle*:
Start at the Ticket Office / Woodland Sculptures / Giant's Adventure Trail , West Lawn / Valentines / The Jungle, Georgian Ride / Insect Hotel / Lost Valley / Charcoal kilns, Yonder Lantavy / Eastern Drive / Sunken Lane – STEWARD'S HOUSE CAFÉ.
Return via The Gardens.

This tour can be done in reverse if you are starting from the Steward's House. It is not for the faint-hearted in either direction!

TOUR 1
Main Garden Features

Route marked on map on front flap
(The Gardens only)

If Squire Jack were your host today, he would be escorting you from his elegant home straight into his gardens on their southern boundary; but those gates are now closed. Instead, **from the Ticket Office**, **cross the Main Drive with care** and enter the The Gardens on their north western boundary. Not so much else has changed though...

FLORA'S GREEN

Proceed straight ahead at the first cross-roads within The Gardens and within seconds the vista of Flora's Green is before you. Here we can take time to set the scene for you a century ago, which we endeavour to reflect and consolidate in our activities around the site today. Though the Industrial Revolution in Horticulture had been in progress since the early 19th century and heating technologies were advanced by 1914, the use of petrol driven machinery would not have been common-place at this time. One of the contemporary hall-marks of Heligan is our focus on labour-intensive, human skills and strength and hand-crafted, non-mechanical processes wherever possible. Flora's Green is one of the few places we condone the use of machinery; for the lawn mower was invented back in the 1840s and there is nothing more evocative of a perfect summer's day than the sweet smell of fresh grass clippings.

Witch's Broom on an old Douglas Fir, an unusual Bonsai feature

Surrounding this grassy sward – and stunning in the spring, as the various crimsons peak and fade on enormous clouds of foliage around this otherwise green enclave – the 'Camellias and Rhododendrons introduced to Heligan pre-1920' form a collection now nationally recognised by Plant Heritage. Many were established during the early years of John Tremayne's tenure and they remain some of the garden's most treasured features, including those raised from original material collected by Sir Joseph Hooker in 1851.

Their care is our priority and indeed our greatest challenge, for many rhododendrons are particularly susceptible to the recently identified fungi, *Phytophthora ramorum* and *Phytophthora kernoviae*. These diseases have in recent years affected woodland and wild rhododendron (and increasingly, other garden shrubs), particularly throughout the mild, damp South West. Heligan's brooding collection also lines the paths encircling both Flora's Green and her whole productive heart (immediately to the south) – but sadly, in gradually depleting numbers. Just as John Tremayne was interested in the science of growing, today's team have been working both with the government department, Fera, to investigate control treatments for the diseases and with Duchy College, Camborne, to secure a future for these veteran specimens. The relatively new technique of micropropagation has created another generation from many of our most valuable individuals... but nothing can replace this awesome, fragile spectacle within our lifetimes.

The Tremayne family nurtured these shrubs to maturity (along with specimen conifers in the vicinity – a

Jack Tremayne took portraits of some of his plant collection for national publication, including in The Gardener's Chronicle, *1896*

Sequoiadendron sempervirens remains in the north-eastern corner and a Witch's Broom on a Douglas Fir *(Pseudotsuga menziesii)* to the south); but they could never have conceived the unique and soulful atmosphere evolving a century on, that we are privileged to enjoy for a little longer.

Traditionally Flora's Green would have hosted celebrations and local events.
Photo © Steve Tanner/Wildworks 100: The Day Our World Changed, August 2014

Kitchen Garden

Pass through a large gateway set within the tall hedge of *Thuja plicata* that runs along the southern edge of Flora's Green. Though this is a new planting, most of the avenue of tall palms in front of it is original, along with the western boundary laurel hedge (to your right, within). The infrastructure of paths and metalwork within the Kitchen Garden is all new – only the inherited well-conditioned soil and the sense of ongoing, timeless, seasonal activity remain from the past. This meticulously managed garden, replicating the very best of past practice and mathematical precision, stands in stark contrast to the brooding presence of the historic shrubs beyond.

Here the Head Gardener of old held sway, only answerable to the Squire in terms of resourcing all the fruit, herb, flower and vegetable requirements of the kitchen, for his family and constant stream of guests. Throughout the Victorian period, the squires held significant civic positions and were obliged to offer regular hospitality. Hence, the delivery of the seedsman's new catalogues each year was eagerly awaited to enhance prestige – while the apprentices arrived and departed with equal regularity.

The specifically labour intensive restoration of these productive gardens during the 1990s was based on the reported evidence that 23 outdoor staff were in employment here in 1914. However, more recently available censuses suggest that, at most, only six were regularly employed as gardeners! The productive gardens you witness today are therefore an unique living example of best practice and maximum production around the year, that would not have been customary a century ago on estates of this size. As a consequence, the modern-day reputation of productive Heligan has been based not on strict replication of its own past (for which

Antirrhinums 'Florists Mixed' and 'Greenhouse Mixed'.

there is minimal archive) but on a summary of the breadth of skills and cropping found anywhere in Britain at the time.

We have our First Horticultural Director, Philip McMillan Browse, to thank for his in-depth research into the precise cultivation techniques of the Edwardian period and for sourcing the hundreds of different traditional varieties of fruit, vegetable, salad and herb that you may see being sown, grown and harvested – or consumed – here today. His seminal publication, *The Heligan Vegetable Bible*, summarised this epic achievement. The restoration crop planting is based on a date of about 1910; so, many of the crops now grown would have found a place here a century ago. In a few cases, none are available back to this date, so slightly more modern cultivars are used.

One of Heligan's chief contemporary purposes is to champion and conserve heritage varieties and we trust that others will be inspired to share in our mission when they spot unusual crops – or better still, when they taste them.

No photographs have come to light of the old Kitchen Garden at Heligan pre-1950, by which time it appears to have been in the care of a single gardener after another period of wartime neglect from 1940. The interesting shape of today's territory, defined by three hedges and a curved wall on the southern boundary, mirrors that first recorded on the 1839 Tithe Map for the Parish of St. Ewe during the tenure of John Hearle Tremayne.

Since clearance during 1992-93 using mechanical equipment, the ground here has been worked, once again, entirely by hand. Though abandoned for some decades prior to discovery, we inherited a soil conditioned over several working lifetimes, which was quickly returned to productivity. A new regime including the regular application of organic matter and plenty of double digging has been in place again for over twenty years, with crops rotated around six plots of 100ft. x 45ft., on a six-year cycle. Vegetable crop families include 1) Potatoes (followed the same year by Winter Brassicas on the same plot), 2) Roots, 3) Legumes, 4) Alliums, 5) Cucurbits and 6) Miscellaneous. There is also a seventh plot of similar dimensions that in itself accommodates a further rotation of crops, including the unbeatable Royal Sovereign strawberries. Their superb flavour reminds us how far modern horticulture has travelled in compliance with European legislation and how diminished is our contemporary satisfaction from today's markets.

The annual rotation of crops described above helps to break the cycle of pests and diseases. Far from embracing the traditional use of 'widow-maker' sprays, we operate on quasi-organic principles, only resorting to the use of chemicals to protect a very few endangered varieties.

Every crop row is labelled in the ground; trained fruit is tagged. The old names are evocative of a past world, encouraged back out of memory to live again. Traditional activities which mark the passage of the year are recognised with joy by many today; while we hope that the opportunity for younger visitors to witness all the stages in cultivation and to meet those who work here will also leave a lasting mark.

Pass on down through the tunnel of traditional apple varieties, the earliest-flowering planted at the top to avoid the frost pocket at the bottom. Very early May is usually the best time to enjoy this iconic scene.

Melon Yard

You enter the heart of The Gardens; witness the regular, more-or-less familiar pulse of generations – an essay in productivity. Here the tiny working buildings are ranged along inside the south wall facing you and around to the west. Clockwise, they are: the Old Tool Shed, Potting Shed, Lean-to, Bothy with Mushroom House below and Fruit Store above – and in the top corner, the doorway into the old Thunderbox Room, where past staff left their names... and from thence departed to the battlefronts. This is where we come to pay our respects, not just on Remembrance Sunday but every single day. Our tribute is giving new life to this old garden; returning structure to function and rediscovering that balance with nature which enables us to work successfully with the ebb and flow of the seasons and nurture the myriad cycles of life. There is now also a formal cast iron plaque, as an enduring tribute.

In the main, all the old garden structures have been restored from total dereliction back to full function – apart from three evocative old boilers you may spot as you follow this tour. Each was originally installed to heat a different glasshouse. They date to different periods. It has proved impossible to genuinely return any of them to original function, although much research and discussion has taken place among horticultural specialists!

We endeavour largely to operate without trace of modern materials or techniques, but the spirit of the Head Gardener has always been to welcome new ideas. Today, without those original boilers, we have to be open about our dependence on some contemporary propagation methods in order to deliver such a cornucopia of produce all year round. Were we to remove the electric heat mats now used over winter and in early spring at the far end of the Melon House

Melon House and Pineapple Pit in spring sunshine, with the original Swan's Egg Pear in blossom

we would be substantially reduced to waiting until the soil was warm enough for direct sowing in the Kitchen Garden, delaying early harvests considerably and thus preventing catch-cropping as well. Our volume and range of harvested crops would be very much reduced – and though this might better replicate past practice here (which served a far smaller 'household'), it would significantly curtail the current horticultural interest around the year for both our visitors and our staff.

Hence, the Melon House, the only glasshouse here, is used around the year – traditionally, to propagate melons during the late summer months (when the fruits are strung in little nets) and also earlier, when a massive harvest of cucumbers is normally achieved. Prior to this, however, throughout the winter and early spring, much of the space is given over to contemporary propagation techniques, germinating vast quantities of seed sown in light-weight, space-saving, cheap plastic trays... Today's staff have searched their souls; they do not want to confuse or deceive their audience by undertaking this critical operation 'behind the scenes'; nor can they realistically adapt it back to traditional technologies, using wholly traditional materials. The volume of clay pots required would fill the whole of this garden and be impossible to handle, even with our large team.

The derelict boiler behind the Melon House is a Horseshoe Boiler, excavated in 1990; volunteers having discovered a half-full bucket of coal under a blanket of overgrowth, placed ready at the top of the silted steps and left for tomorrow – perhaps nearly a century ago.

The original heating system for the run of large pits in front of the Melon House is somewhat different! An earlier technology... After excavation, the structure was eventually identified as a Pineapple Pit, traditionally fired by freshly rotting horse manure heaped into the pigeon-holed trenches to front and rear. Of course, in the early-mid nineteenth century, draught horses were the only form of haulage, so accessing this material in vast quantities was not a problem. Now however, restoration to full function has proved challenging, because of the dearth of quality material! We grow Pineapples 'Smooth Cayenne' and 'Jamaica Queen' and, with experimentation still at the heart of the exercise, have had some luck in bringing these old varieties to fruit on a number of occasions with delicious results. It appears that this skill was never one of the Tremaynes' recognised horticultural triumphs, for in the early Victorian era Heligan's name did not appear on the prize lists of the Royal Horticultural Society of Cornwall in this respect at all!

Heligan Pineapple
'Jamaica Queen'
Photo © Clay Perry

The remaining frames (note, all with their beaver-tail glazing – *described later*) also contribute to the massive propagation and production schedule around the year, with most of our crops being delivered by barrow as freshly harvested ingredients for our own Heligan Kitchen - 457 yards from soil to plate!

The beautiful curved wall that scoops up the sun from the south tells a story all of its own. Built largely of stone over a period of time, the south-facing aspect is of brick, in order to better absorb the heat and ripen the trained fruit. Zinc plant labels naming specific varieties were discovered in the vicinity during the early restoration and hundreds of nail holes can still be seen in the old lime mortar. The 1907 map (*on the front flap*) shows a structure of some sort on the western half of this wall (possibly open-fronted most of the year?). Cropping would no doubt have been substantial, hence the adjacent Fruit Store.

Of the working buildings, the Potting Shed nestling in the south-west corner still represents the pulse of the whole garden – an essay in productivity; with the door always half-ajar and the pervading rich aroma of compost within. Here seeds are sown and later pricked out to be grown on elsewhere, crops potted for forcing, harvests gathered, flowers dried. How many generations have practised these routines here?

A single original fruit tree stands sentinel to the southern gateway – a Swan's Egg Pear. The fruits are harvested with long-handled pruners and caught in nets. It is no longer a commercial variety, but was traditionally used to make the delicious drink, Perry.

Signatures on the wall
Photo © Charles Francis

Potting Shed - workplace of generations

Bee Boles and Head Gardener's Office

Let us continue on through, and down beside the Bee Bole Lawn. The early Victorian walled structure to your left is designed to accommodate two rows of seven barley-straw bee skeps – sited in close proximity to the Kitchen Garden in order to promote pollination of the crops. This is a relatively early design for honey-bee hives; inefficient in that the bees had to be smoked out and killed in order for their wax and honey to be collected. Hence new swarms had to be introduced every year. We now use more modern hives out in the estate, beyond the Wildlife Hide; while encouraging some of the many other bees to occupy crevices nearby.

A little further, on your right, and overhung by a veteran from the Hooker Collection (*Rhododendron falconeri* – raised from original, 1851 seed), you will come upon the Head Gardener's Office. It is built against the back wall of the Flower Garden, which is itself testament to successive heating technologies employed since the glasshouses on its south-facing side were first constructed. Duck your head as you proceed into the building and soak up the atmosphere. The relic of an old Britannia Boiler (model 2-K) remains at the bottom of a long flight of steps, purchased by Jack Tremayne in 1908. In the far room, the last Head Gardener's kettle (discovered in derelict situ in 1990) remains on the cill by the hearth, along with his mug.

Returning outside, an old gardener's bothy and a tiny (north-facing!) Banana House confront you as you approach the door into the Flower Garden.

Bee Bole Lawn

Above: *a century-old stroll with pet dogs, under the* Rhododendron falconeri *outside the Head Gardener's Office; Here, the same building restored, today*

Photo © Toby Strong

The Library of Heligan House adorned with flowers, about 1900

Today's source of supply – the Flower Garden… in June

Flower Garden

There is no greater joy than to arrive in here on a warm summer's afternoon, with the butterflies and bees hovering along waves of scented blooms on a gentle breeze. This feast of colour and artistry is, by its nature, transient, disappearing back into the ground later in the year. Though mostly period-correct, none of it is original planting. The seasonal contrast is dramatic... again, master-minded by Philip McMillan Browse; with as much time still spent on back-breaking double-digging as on delicate harvest activities. A century ago, Jack Tremayne's Flower Garden was more exotic in its plantings – but no record of it whatsoever was available at the time of the restoration here, in 1994.

Views from opposite ends, a century apart

This exhilarating space, an annual essay in the ebb and flow of life, is enclosed by a great and graceful framework of historic importance, telling its own story from around 1800. The walled garden, listed Grade II by English Heritage, was constructed of imported Flemish bricks. They can be dated by size; smallest are oldest. During the early nineteenth century, the China Clay industry north of St. Austell was exporting in bulk to the potteries of the Low Countries; boats would then return to new local harbours with these bricks... for use within the many 'country seats' nearby. This garden is, unusually, trapezoid in shape. As in the Melon Yard, the all-important purpose was to create a warm, sheltered area for cultivation. Early crops of flowering corms, salads, herbs and vegetables thrive in open ground and their proximity to the back door of Heligan House used to facilitate immediate delivery of tender items.

The large range of almost south-facing glass incorporates possibly the last remaining Paxton House in Britain, dating back to the 1860s. Designed by Joseph Paxton and originally sold as a flat-pack, it would have been commonly seen in the mid-Victorian era. The Britannia Boiler in the Head Gardener's Office would have been its most recent source of heat; witness the old pipework. It has been restored as a Vinery, full of traditional dessert grape varieties. At the far end is a Citrus House... with all fruits specifically propagated for special occasions in the Squire's dining room! The beaver-tail glazing style (found also in the Melon Yard) is designed to direct the flow of rain water down the centre of each pane, thus discouraging rot in the timber framework. However, maintenance operations here definitely remain Forth Bridge style, with permanently employed painters and carpenters still part of the outdoor team.

To the immediate left as you enter the main door into this garden there is significant erosion to the brickwork. Some suggest this is due to the noxious chemicals used inside a lean-to glasshouse that was dismantled many years ago. It may have been an Orchid House. In 1990, on discovery of this then derelict garden, yet another presumably replacement, free-standing structure, was discovered here beneath the overgrowth. This may have been the Carnation House mentioned in the 1914 Labour Books. The hope is that we may eventually be able to complete the restoration here, by adding back a fourth range of glass for another traditional collection of contemporary interest.

To your left, on the far wall facing south-south west, is the Peach House. This is likely not to have been constructed until at least the 1880s, because it has more modern glazing in larger sheets, which allow in more light. Note a blocked up doorway in its back wall... a mystery for later. The fruiting of the beautifully fan-trained trees within represents the height of summer joy, after all their time-consuming care around the year.

Finally, the original pot-boy's Dipping Pool is still set at the centre of the garden, receiving rain water not only from the gutters of the glasshouses but also from most of the drains in the gardens. Maintaining the proper functioning of this mostly invisible network, below ground, is perhaps the most important aspect of all our garden activities.

Cosmos, Cornflower, Clarkia, Larkspur and Love-in-a-mist...

Traditional varieties of dessert grapes returned to the Vinery

Sundial & Scented Gardens

By comparison with the dearth of archive concerning the productive gardens at Heligan, the 'Sun-Dial Garden' (previously known as 'Mrs Tremayne's Flower Garden') is relatively well documented. It was named after Squire John Tremayne's wife, Mary, who may have designed and possibly helped plant it. It achieved national acclaim in 1896 in a December issue of *The Gardeners' Chronicle*, when commentator J. Roberts described it as approaching his own ideal of an old English flower garden.

It remains a challenge to match that achievement, and a selection of archival photos taken between 1908 and the 1950s have presented numerous design and planting options in terms of restoration period. We have opted for a largely pre-Jekyll selection and tailored it to the Cornish climate.

The proximity of this garden to Heligan House meant that it became the final area to slip into nature's embrace. Thus, some treasured original plant specimens remain... the fragile Handkerchief Tree (*Davidia involucrata*) at the top of the lawn probably dates back to 1905 – Jack would have purchased it from Veitch's Nursery soon after introduction from China. Its white bracts in May are an unusual sight, followed by round, inedible fruits. From under its boughs you can look across to the west, over the walls of the Flower Garden, to enjoy a bank of colour on more massive rhododendrons in spring. On the outer wall of the Flower Garden is an original climber, *Stauntonia hexaphylla*, which

has an unusual, evergreen compound leaf formation and still vigorous habit. Close-by is the wisteria-clad stone gateway back into the Flower Garden; May is the month for its scented splendour too.

Immediately after World War I, Jack spent a few more swan-song years at Heligan and in 1920 invited architect H. G. Kitchen to design some gates for this southern entrance. Above, a gentleman poses stylishly beside the subsequent finished installation! These decorative cast iron gates featuring a grape-vine motif were removed during World War II for safe-keeping.

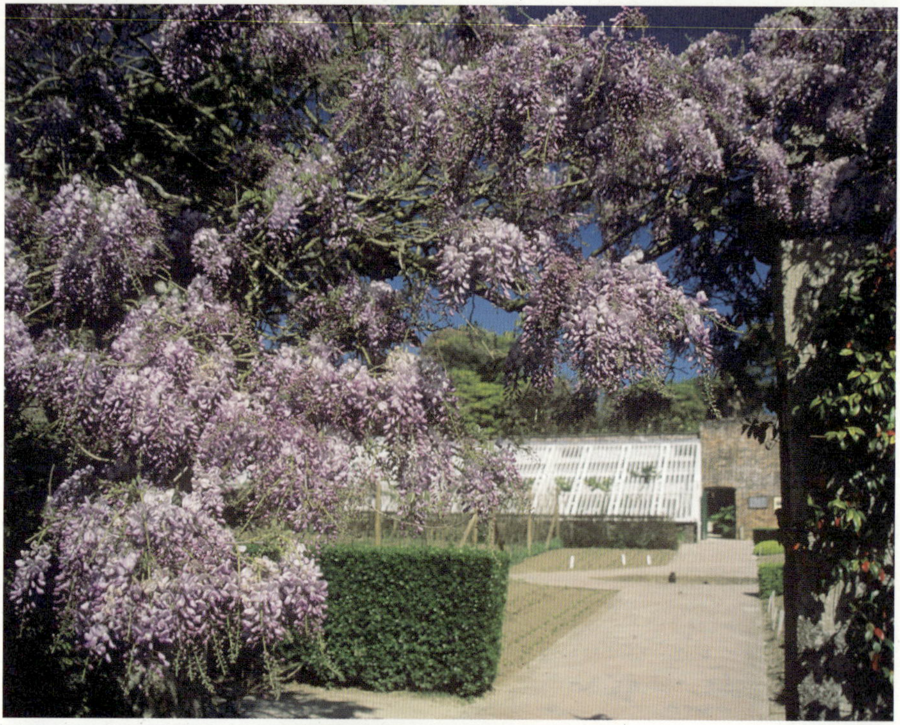

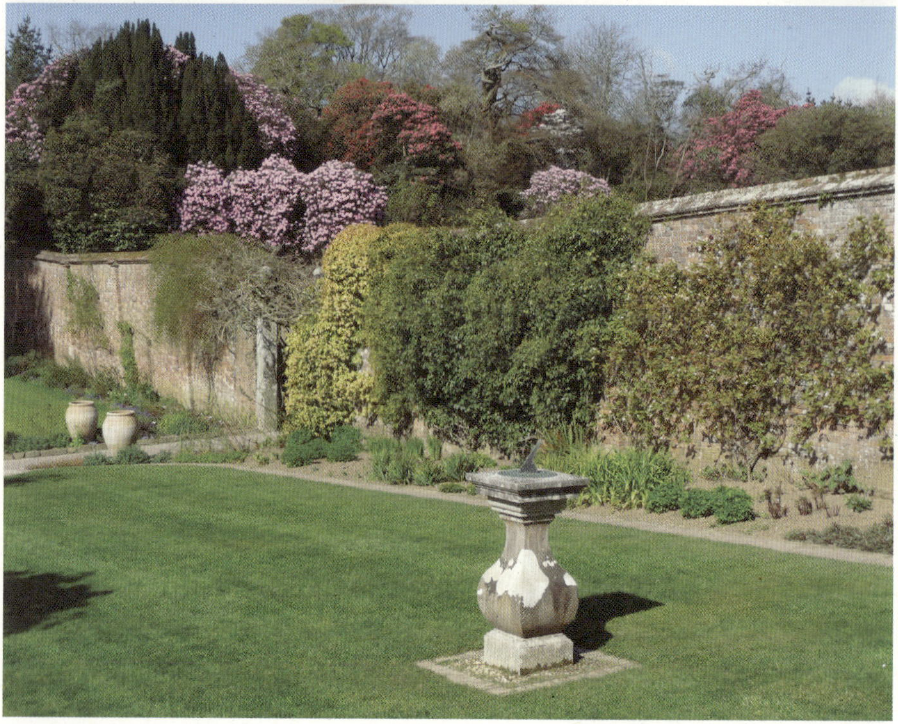

The old Handkerchief Tree also known as 'Dove' or 'Ghost' Tree now creates a shady corner for a memorial bench, from which to view the Sundial Garden and the rhododendrons of Sikkim

Sikkim

A poignant corner remains to the east, beyond the Scented Garden, close to the boundary laurel. The headstones of the old Pets' Graveyard were discovered early in the restoration. From the dates, these must have been pets belonging to Jack Tremayne and his parents... TOTO; TINY 1873; LULU 1890; WINKIE 1894 and JUMBO APRIL 1892 AGED 15 YEARS...

Proceed on, up into the heavy shade.

Your tour now takes you into an untamed land... around some incredible stands of old rhododendrons whose high blooms are best enjoyed in April from the top of the Sundial Lawn, or from within the Flower Garden. Access is difficult up the path running outside the western wall of the Flower Garden, but the gaunt imagery is haunting. These specimens are growing in pretty much indigenous, feral habit. Whichever route you take, imbibe this fragile splendour imported from the Himalaya over 150 years ago. One or two infected with Sudden Oak Death have recently been cut back to base, to encourage healthy regeneration.

Pencalenick Greenhouse

Back in civilization, a crimson haze of a different, meticulously tended kind... this collection of Victorian Pelargoniums offers year-round interest because of the care it receives, almost daily. Within, you will also spot succulent aeoniums and the velvety purple-flowering *Tibouchina urvillleana*... a South American treat for our off-season. The glasshouse itself was offered to Heligan during the 1990s by Pencalenick School, which occupies another famed Cornish seat from the Victorian era. There, beside the Tresillian River near Truro in the 1840s, was a pineapple competitor and later, an Italian Garden. Heligan was not alone locally in its fashionable endeavours. John Nelson dismantled, transported and reconstructed the building here. Due north from the adjacent cross-roads, and still enclosed by its original boundary laurel is...

Italian Garden

This secret place was Jack's retreat, built around 1906. He may have converted the summerhouse from an existing working building... into an enclave for relaxation, facing south and themed to his beloved Italy. The two original Kiwi fruit (*Actinidia chinensis*) would have been relatively new to Britain when planted (introduced to Britain by E. H. (Chinese) Wilson – of Veitch provenance). The statue is a replica of 'Putto with a Dolphin', first supplied from a mould by Verocchio and recently sourced again from the original foundry near Florence. Here, Jack escaped the present and contemplated the future – he moved to live in Italy in 1923. No doubt in its first form this garden would have enjoyed more sunshine and plants from more arid climates would have thrived. The stone slabs around the pool were originally loose, with herbs planted underfoot.

Today this garden stands as somewhat of a tribute to the memory of the extraordinary man who restored it in 1991, first bringing Heligan to national attention; John Nelson (V.M.M.).

Western Ride and The Ravine

Photo courtesy of C. Tyler

Jack Tremayne's photos from before World War 1 vividly capture his chosen plant palette

Due north of the Italian Garden, stretching upward behind the summerhouse, this area remains one of the on-going, unsettled mysteries of Heligan. No doubt conceived by Jack as an extension of his continental dream, a fashionable Alpine Ravine as such would have dated back to the 1890s; however the OS map of 1907 shows nothing of the dramatic relief of this place today. Instead, at that time in this location was a formal garden of beds on flat ground and there is even a photo of it. Hence, we have to assume that this was possibly the last garden Jack constructed before World War 1, with the eye-level water course supplied by his new Ram pump, installed in 1908. The old photos show young rhododendrons in place and a metal detector survey has unearthed original plant labels. This is being completely replanted for 2017, including a new water feature.

Western Ride, an original route, runs due north back up to today's Garden Entrance. It is lined with original rhododendrons and camellias - and their progeny - and tall palms (*Trachycarpus fortunei*), and echoes the photos from a century ago. Near to the top of the path, turn left for a comfort break!

Chart of Seasonal Delights

	Dec.	January	February	March	April	May	J
Northern Gardens							
Flowering Trees & Shrubs		→ Camellia —TO MAY		Magnolia campbelli Drimys winterii →	Davidia involucrata Halesia Azalea	Cor Plag beti
				Rhododendron —TO MAY			
Climbers			Hamamelis Hardenbergia —PEACH HOUSE		Embothrium Wisteria		
Perennials		Hellebore Cyclamen	Daffodil Bergenia Snowdrops	Primula	Euphorbia Lily of the Valley	Paeony	De
Fruit				Peach blossom Quince blossom	Pear blossom Apple blosso	St	
		DOUBLE DIGGING		Rhubarb			
Vegetables		Winter brassicas	Curly Kale	Chicory Sprouting broccoli	Sea Kale Radish	Asparagus	
Cut flowers		Anemone de Caen —MAR.		Iris Narcissus Ranunculus →	← Lettuce → Doronicum Wallflower Sweet William	Early pe Cama Stoc	An
Jungle Exotics, Flowering Trees & Shrubs		Acacia bakeyana Protea —TO MAR.	Hamamelis Rhododendron —TO MAY Clematis armandii	Magnolia Soulangeana Skunk cabbage	Echium Crinodendron Tree fern Gunnera manicata Fuchsia microphy	Cornus k Trac	
Wider Estate			Primroses COPPICING Catkins TREE SURGERY/PLANTING	Calves Chicks CHARCOAL BURNING —	Lambs Ducklings OCT.	Bluebells fox Campions	Ho
Wildlife		Snowdrops Tawny owls —PAIR Queen wasps & bees —EMERGE Charms of finches flocking —	Dawn Chorus Barn owls —PAIR	Goslings Swallows, Martins, Goldfinch Chaffinch Greenfinch	Longtail tits Swift Butterfly Dragonfly	Frogle Lin x B	

JULY	AUGUST	SEPTEMBER	OCTOBER	NOVEMBER	DECEMBER	JAN.
...s capitata — FLOWERS	→	FRUITS	Acer - FOLIAGE			
...NDIAL GDN.	Hoheria Magnolia delavayi		Disanthus			
...nthus Eucryphia ←	Fuchsia	→	Callicarpa - BERRIES			
...inus	← Hydrangea	→				
	← Clerodendrum	→				
	Mandevilla laxa					
Rose	Clianthus	Cobaea scandens				
...hinium	Lily Verbena bonariensis	Nerine		Cyclamen →		
Agapanthus		Montbretia	SEAWEED — VEG. GARDEN			
...wberry Rasps.	Melon Grape	Pineapple		Citrus		
...e Gooseberry	Japanese wineberry	Quince		DOUBLE DIGGING		
Peach Currants	Pear	Fig	Passion fruit — FLOWERS JULY			
Peas & Beans ←	Apples →	Kohl Rabi	Leeks Brussels			
	Chard — TO NOV. Aubergine	Cucurbit		Winter Roots		
...atoes Globe arti.	Peppers	Chillies	Jerusalem artichoke			
...sia Black poppy	Zinnia	Rudbeckia	Anemone de Caen			
Sweet pea	Scabious	Helychrysum				
...rhinum Cosmos	Cleome Dahlia	Chrysanthemum				
...sa — FLOWERS	FRUIT Banana	Kiwi fruit	Acacia bakeyana			
...lygala myrtifolia	Nymphaea	Hedychium	Mahonia			
...carpus Agapanthus africanus			Protea			
TO OCT. Lobelia Canna	Myrtle — TO OCT.		Leonotis Leonurus			
...a tupa	Acanthus mollis		POND CLEARANCE			
...loves Hydrangea — TO OCT.	Sweet chestnuts		BRAMBLE CLEARANCE			
...EY EXTRACTION HAYMAKING			COPPICING TREE SURGERY TREE PLANTING			
Wild Iris	Orchard fruit	Autumn colour	Jungi			
...lderflowers	Kingfisher — TO APRIL			Brambling		
...d Hummingbird hawkmoth	Snipe Linnet					
Blue tits/Sparrows — NEST	Mushrooms & Toadstools					
...otted flycatcher Grasshoppers & Crickets			Winter berries			
...n owl chicks ←	→ fledge	Redwing Fieldfare				

TOUR 2 – Curiosities
Route marked on map on front flap

From the Garden Entrance, return to join Western Ride, but this time head north (turn left at the cross-roads inside The Gardens). We now take you on a tour of some more unusual, individual features. Before the big green gates, turn right onto Beacon Path.

This short section is not an original route, but soon links in with the old perimeter path inside the original boundary wall, dating back to the early 1800s. In places, you can see the pastures beyond.

The magnificent magnolia is at least a century-old *Magnolia campbellii*. It still flowers profusely, most years in early March; but not in all. We view it as our harbinger of spring.

THE MOUNT

Continue along Beacon Path and The Mount is before you on the right-hand side, with its spiral path winding to the top. Here, the field beyond the perimeter wall of The Gardens has been recorded as Beacon Field from as long ago as 1623, so we are persuaded the structure is an utilitarian relic dating back to the time of the Spanish Armada. The view from the top of this mound would at that time have been uninterrupted, across open ground, to the coast.

Continue along this circular path, past veteran and juvenile Heligan rhododendrons and camellias, until the view opens up before you.

NORTHERN SUMMERHOUSE

This structure was the first to have been built in the new pleasure grounds by Henry Hawkins Tremayne, in the very early nineteenth century... it features on the 1839 Tithe Map of St. Ewe. The bricks match the oldest in the Flower Garden and the view would have thrilled morning riders, looking right across St. Austell Bay to the Gribben, proud of Fowey – and to South Devon on a clear day. The beautiful brick and cobble floor inside the summerhouse is original, while the slate paving around the new pool has been borrowed from the old stone hunting dog kennels, sited behind the hedge in the middle distance, across Higher Beef Park.

Eastern Ride

Heligan, New Zealand

Depart the enclosed Northern Summerhouse Garden through the opposite gateway and join Eastern Ride, the very first route constructed by Henry Hawkins Tremayne, before 1776. Turn left and head south. Some very early camellias remain. This path has been resurfaced and lined with a traditional cobbled gulley, which directs the majority of the rainfall straight off the gravel surface into a system of underground pipes, feeding rainwater eventually down into the Jungle valley.

A collection of interesting original plantings from around the world still lines Eastern Ride.

From the top, they include, alternately on right and left: the weeping, feathery evergreen *Podocarpus salignus* from South America; summer-flowering evergreen, *Eucryphia cordi-folia*; the beautiful sprawling and twice-flowering *Magnolia soulangeana* 'Lennei' and upright, Chinese, *Ginkgo biloba* – as well as numerous old azaleas, rhododendrons, and Chusan Palms (*Trachycarpus fortunei*).

New Zealand

Several detours to the right, off Eastern Ride, exhibit a substantial array of New Zealand plants, including a magnificent collection of old Tree Ferns (*Dicksonia antarctica*) and a newer one, carved by Maori chiefs and imported in recent years. There is also a splendid, original specimen of summer-flowering *Magnolia delavayi* and, if you keep your sight-line raised, some impressive old palms. There is a very settled, organic feel to this whole garden, although most of the planting at the top (northern end) is a whole century younger than that at the bottom.

New Zealand plants tend to have coarse, textural foliage, some with an interlacing habit which deters native animals from eating them. *Muehlenbeckia complexa* is a recent such planting. There are a number of interesting ground cover plants here too, including the grass *Chionocloa flavicans* and miniature Alpine ferns, *Leptinella minor* and *Leptinella calcarea*. Other oddities are the Tree Fuchsia (*Fuchsia excorticata*) - the largest fuchsia in the world, as well as *Fuchsia procumbens*, the smallest! No wonder the old Head Gardener was proud to be photographed in this garden.

THE GROTTO

These structures (detours to your left as you pass on down Eastern Ride) are romantic features typical of the early Victorian period. The Grotto was probably constructed using quartz encrusted granite hewn from Bodmin Moor. One can but imagine its original pure beauty, especially by candle-light. Moss and lichen suitably complement its contrasting atmosphere today. The capping stone over the old 'well' may have come from St. Ewe Church; this elaborate decoration belying the fact that this water feature formed part of the essential garden drainage system.

At the very bottom of Eastern Ride you can peep around to the right and spot the early Victorian Bee Bole wall at the top of a concealed lawn, described on Tour 1. Now, however, head straight on due south towards the north-eastern corner of the walls of the Flower Garden, where a small green door opens back into that glorious space, with a small boiler house outside. You will spot in the gloaming down another small flight of steps a rare, derelict Weeks' Upright Tubular Boiler, dating back to the 1840s. Impossible to restore, part of it was recently discovered down in an old dump on the estate and returned to situ.

Photo © Charles Francis

Reserve Yards

Now head into the two Reserve Yards outside the eastern wall of the Flower Garden. The current lay-out of these enclosed spaces dates back at least to 1880. In the first, restored frames with superb ironwork are used to bring on young plants for the productive gardens. The protected ground is also ideal for overwintering freshly planted pots of spring bulbs. We grow dozens of varieties afresh every autumn and then set the terracotta pots around the whole site as they come into bud on a schedule from December to April. Used bulbs are then planted out in the Stewards House Garden, where there is an increasing display every year. We have plans to develop new herbaceous borders against the sunny walls here, in order to demonstrate the traditional uses of both medicinal and culinary herbs.

Proceed on through to the next outdoor 'room', with far more mystery in its remains. We are convinced this space was originally used for domesticated animals. The essay writ upon the surrounding walls in terms of old roof lines and earlier apertures sets the imagination racing, and the seven blocked arches evident on the left-hand wall mirror the maths of the Bee Boles. The cobbled floor criss-crossed with gulleys suggests that the animals housed were not insubstantial – possibly veal calves, accommodated in a long lean-to on the outer side of the wall. Retrace your steps and head around to your right, to take your own guess...

Wishing Well

On your way, pass an original well which supplied both house and gardens with water, over centuries. It was excavated to a considerable depth by volunteers back in the 1990s – the current structure above ground is largely new.

Now head out beyond The Gardens (past another dovecote) and into the eastern side of The Estate. Here, some of the essential traditional working features have recently been built from scratch, as close to their original locations as possible. (Mainly, this is because they used to be sited on what is now separately owned ground, behind the old walls that run down on your right, and have been converted for domestic use.)

Sawmill and Workshop

The woods at Heligan would have been a substantial source of material for all sorts of jobs within and beyond the Heligan Estate. There was a woodsman and several carpenters on the books in 1914, who seem to have commanded the highest wages, with such responsibilities as repairing the 'Houses' (glasshouses) as well as the Squire's 'Yacht'. From 1914 the eastern shelterbelt of conifers cocooning The Gardens was decimated to harvest timber for the war effort. Today, good quality Heligan timber becomes available both for construction and crafts on a fairly regular basis, as storms continue to take their toll and from time to time dangerous specimens have to be removed. Some of these might also be unusual species, creating special opportunities for today's Workshop.

The original hand-saw pit was located not far from here together with, after the war, an engine-driven circular Sawmill. Today we run an electrically powered planking machine and occasionally import steam power as well. The story of a tree, even from its delivery here, is an interesting one, as every subject is assessed for its best use. Our team consider each trunk for construction, carpentry and wood-turning purposes and plank accordingly. We have a kiln-drying facility, which can condition and hasten the readiness of the timber.

Green (or fresh) Heligan Wood is sometimes used for wood-turning, incorporating the natural edge, or bark. It is then left to air-dry over a period of months, before final sanding and oil treatment. These pieces have unique appeal and are sold from our Heligan Shop.

Steward's House

This makes an ideal base from which to access The Estate. It is an elegant dwelling built during the mid-nineteenth century for the steward of the Heligan Estate and it is now Grade II listed. There is a Café here for garden visitors, open during the main season, and what was once a field outside now offers a beautifully secluded garden, picnic and play area and toilet facilities, open all year round.

TOUR 3 – *Animals*

Pale Green areas shown on map inside front cover are usually accessible to visitors

For centuries the Home Farm was an essential part of the self-sufficient estate and it is clear that the Squires Tremayne took a keen interest in their livestock long before they created the gardens, keeping personal records of their animals and buying and selling individuals of good pedigree from neighbouring estates. Henry Hawkins Tremayne was a founder member of the Royal Cornwall Agricultural Association in 1793 and of course, soon after, was judged to have the best bull. His son, John Hearle, is on the record as being passionate about his woods and his farm and his large family inherited these interests. The original Home Farm buildings occupied ground to the immediate north-east of Heligan House; but in recent years most of these have been sold and converted to human habitation – so dry cover for our own livestock has been very limited.

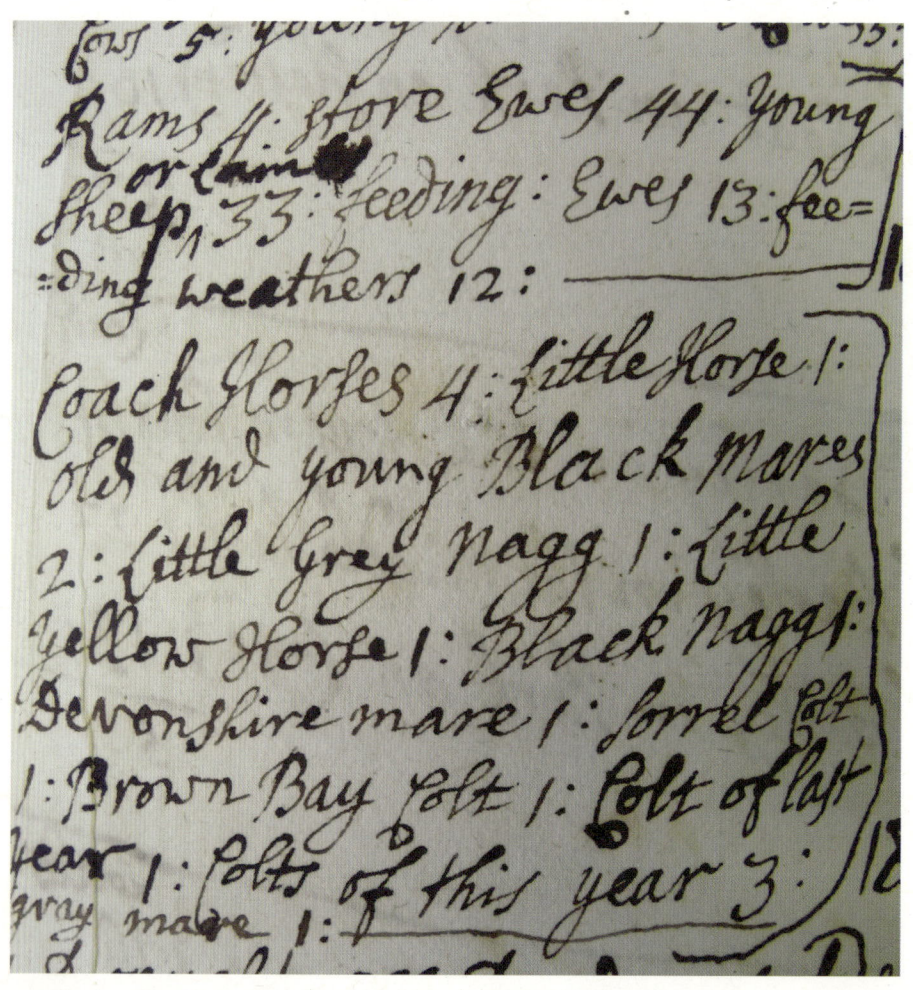

Predominantly this traditional accommodation revolved around the estate's need for large numbers of horses (and associated staff) – for haulage of family carriages and goods carts, as well as for riding and agricultural purposes. (Significant acreage was dedicated to oats to fuel them!) Apart from Heligan House itself, the old stable block, with clock tower on top (visible from the Sundial Garden), is the only other listed building within the now private grounds – not open to visitors. There also used to be a big wagonhouse and storage for a vast array of equine equipment.

Tour 3, using the Steward's House as a base, focuses on both Heligan livestock and the breadth of wildlife that resides or visits here at different times of year. Our desire is to use the Heligan landscape to support a range of traditional breeds and varieties, while providing close-up experiences for you wherever possible as well. This mirrors our ethos in the productive gardens, where our purpose is three-fold: to conserve, to feed and to educate. (Restoring body and soul goes without saying!)

Much of what we have to offer here is accessible to all within a relatively confined area; with Higher Beef Park and Park an Lann used seasonally as our main show fields – when livestock have young with them and/or require more intensive care; leaving this ground to rest intermittently. The outer pastures of The Estate, facing back here from across the valleys, provide additional grazing – and a more challenging circuit for visitors on the far side of Lost Valley (Tour 4).

A page from the accounts of Squire Lewis Tremayne, grandfather of Henry Hawkins Tremayne, details his livestock in 1716-17. Image opposite courtesy CRO, Ref T/1310. *Jack Tremayne had a herd of Jerseys here in the early twentieth century.*

The Barn

This relatively new dry space provides a necessary replacement to the traditional Heligan Home Farm complex and an accessible focus for our expansion into animal husbandry. Here we celebrate the diversity of the gene pool and can now bring you up close to witness our awesome livestock and the associated seasonal agricultural processes as well. For our staff it is a welcome dry cover, enabling them to undertake necessary procedures with greater comfort and efficiency. We hope this opportunity will enhance not only your appreciation of the skills attached to animal husbandry but also, for all generations, the sheer wonder of life in the animal world.

Heavy Horses

In recent years we have been very lucky to have Izzy and Courage make their home here on Heligan Home Farm. They are both Shire Horses, but sourced from different breeders and Courage is still only a few years old – so less experienced in his duties! They generally live outdoors but like company and we graze them in the fields closest to us.

Izzy is well trained in haulage. She will happily pull carts, but where wheeled access is not possible she has the strength and agility to haul large tree trunks out of the woodland valleys and deliver them to our Sawmill for planking. She also pulls a traditional plough to cultivate arable fields here prior to seed sowing.

Izzy harrowing Park-an-Lann

Poultry Orchard

Our poultry are an endless source of entertainment for young and old. We keep chickens, ducks and geese. The birds are not raised for their meat - but our staff enjoy their eggs! We are working towards a collection of pedigree birds, sometimes importing pedigree eggs which can be incubated by our resident Silkies - renowned for doing a good job. Our chicken breeds include Silver-pencilled Plymouth Rock, Wyandotte, Cornish Game – and Marsh Daisy, which is a rare breed. Ducks include Cayuga and Aylesbury which are also rare breeds, plus Call Duck and Indian Runner. We also, as you will hear, keep geese.

Heritage Breeds

In parallel with our ethos in the Productive Gardens, conservation of our heritage and emphasis on flavour go hand in hand with our mission to sustain interest in the skills and knowledge that are fundamental to the pattern and good heart of our countryside. You are free to wander through the pastures that are made accessible to you, at a respectful distance from our livestock. We generally lamb our sheep in early spring, the herds calve in late summer and the pigs usually farrow twice a year.

We have selected a wide range of breeds, more or less rare, but all with a long history of contentment to live and breed outdoors as well as being renowned for their good meat. Our pigs can also sometimes be found foraging in temporary enclosures within woodland areas. Our cows are 'finished' on grass (not grain), which heightens flavour, and we use a local slaughterhouse. Heligan-reared meat features on the Heligan Kitchen menu as often as possible.

Heligan Sheep

Devon and Cornwall Longwools are classed as a Vulnerable Rare Breed, meaning total numbers are in the hundreds only. We are building up our flock, so only the rams not good enough to continue the bloodline go to slaughter (usually at 5-6 months old). The meat is tender and lean. Longwools are placid animals; they have few problems lambing and make excellent mothers.

There have been Longwool sheep in the South West for centuries, coping well outdoors and, unsurprisingly, producing more wool per head than any other breed. Not top quality however, it is used in making carpets, rugs and other home furnishings as well as dolls' hair!

If you see a new lamb outdoors apparently neglected, please do not approach. Its mother will be marking her territory against predators.

Devon & Cornwall Longwool Lamb
Photo: Albert Savage

Hebridean Sheep were until recently classed as an Endangered Breed, but numbers are picking up. These primitive sheep have soft black fleeces, two or four horns and produce fine lean meat.

Herdwicks are seldom seen outside their home territory in the Lake District. They have white heads and legs, long black wool which fades brown in the sun and grey in old age, producing a stunning range of natural colours for woollen rugs and tweeds. They are renowned for their robust health in difficult conditions but ranked low on lambing capacity.

Kerry Hills originate from the English/Welsh borders and until recently were registered as a Rare Breed. However their pretty black markings on head and legs and high quality white wool have made them popular among smallholders. The ewes make excellent mothers and we are working on building up our own flock.

Jacob Sheep are probably the oldest breed in the world. They originate from the Middle East and came to the British Isles in the C16th. Today they have a ready market for their meat, skins, wool and horn. We lamb them in late spring and all the rams go to slaughter.

HELIGAN CATTLE

Dexters originated in South West Ireland and are a Traditional Breed that has found favour in recent years, both for conservation grazing and the high quality of its meat. There are short-legged and non-short-legged versions, both equally endearing.

Highland cattle are one of Britain's oldest and most distinctive breeds and they are doing well today. They are hardy, long-lived and great mothers. Notwithstanding their traditional habitat on poor ground, their marbled meat has an outstanding reputation. Respect is the key word here.

White Park is a Rare Breed, probably the most ancient cattle breed in Britain. Animals are white with black 'points' and long curving horns. They create a magnificent ambience at Heligan.

Highland cow and calf
Photo: Albert Savage

Tamworth sow and piglet
Photo © Toby Strong

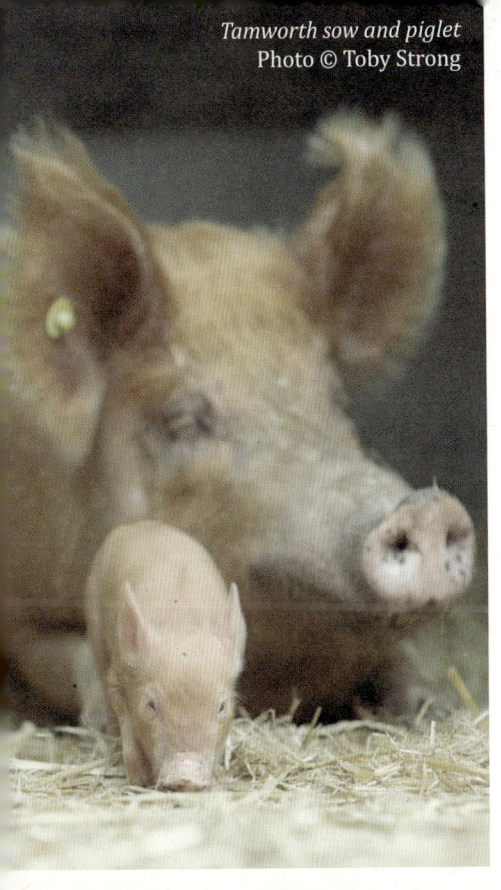

HELIGAN PIGS

Berkshires are new to Heligan in 2017- but the oldest recorded pedigree pig in Britain. They are black with pink noses, feet and tails and produce meat of excellent flavour.

Cornish Blacks are registered as a Vulnerable Rare Breed. There are less than 300 breeding sows remaining in Britain although, as good mothers. these huge animals are renowned for their large and multiple litters. They are Britain's only 'All-Black' pig. They produce great meat, the piglets normally departing at about 5 months.

Tamworths are adorable – no two ways about it – and if you are lucky enough to come across a recent farrow of piglets the experience will certainly make your day! However, they too are still classed 'Vulnerable' by the Rare Breeds Survival Trust, of which Heligan is a member

Tamworth piglets
Photo: Albert Savage

Exotic Pets

As the British Empire expanded, the Victorian and Edwardian eras witnessed the import of not only exotic plants but also exotic pets. There are early photographs of at least one monkey in the gardens and a parrot in the dining room, as well as several of emus – both caged and on the loose! These birds clearly developed a reputation locally... (However, we can be glad the Tremaynes did not opt for far noisier peacocks!) Well, the Heligan emus are back, a century on, in a secure, 6ft high enclosure on the western edge of Parc an Lann, immediately beyond the lower exit from the gardens of the Steward's House.

The emu is the second tallest bird in the world (after the ostrich) and comes from Australia. It cannot fly; but can run at speeds of up to 25mph and is omnivorous! Its eggs are beautiful and edible and are laid from the autumn... up to 40 per year! The male carries out most of the nursery duties, refusing both food and drink while he incubates them for 40 days and then he guards the chicks for the next five to seven months. Emus can live for up to 20 years; our pair are seven years old.

Bees

There are numerous species of bee on site, including the Honey Bee. Some live in wall crevices, others in the soil and yet others in shelters we provide, made of tube-shaped natural materials. They perform a crucial role in pollination and yet are threatened by modern agriculture. As you would expect, Nicotinoids are not used on this site... we must do all we can to support bees.

You may already have spotted the early Victorian Bee Boles adjacent to the Kitchen Garden. This fascinating but inefficient structure is no longer used by our apiarists; instead we have modern hives sited on the edge of Beacon Park. Occasionally swarms can occur anywhere at Heligan and we employ local expertise to maximise these opportunities for additional colonies within The Estate. Visitors are advised to stay at a distance. We are participating in a conservation project to re-establish the Black Bee, whose characteristics are more suited to the British climate than those of the typical Honey Bee. Visit our Bee Observation Hive near the top of Georgian Ride/West, to see them up close.

Macaque Monkey

Heligan Emu 1914

Heligan Emu 2014

Heligan Wildlife

A century ago, our contemporary focus on conservation would have been unusual; while comprehensive knowledge of the natural world would have been commonplace. Wildlife populations were less threatened by chemical applications than by willful shooting, not only for game but to feed the Victorian obsession with taxidermy. How times change! Your experience here today is intended to offer opportunities around the year and across a diversity of habitats, to enhance your knowledge and appreciation without disadvantaging the subjects! The Estate comprises predominantly woodland and pasture, often still separated by traditional Cornish hedges, with areas of wetland adjacent to lakes, leats and streams. In general the oldest woods are in the valleys; newer plantings on higher ground on the western edge of the estate were installed around 1800, to serve as shelterbelts protecting the then nascent gardens. Much has since been replanted.

These varied habitats, as well as the gardens, attract a wide range of mammals, birds, amphibians, reptiles and insects; some commonplace and some quite rare. Our team manages the land in rhythm with their needs as far as possible, sometimes supplementing this with specific plantings to support threatened species. In particular, we have set aside an area close to the Steward's House, where you can particularly focus your interest...

WILDLIFE HIDE

Wildlife abounds at Heligan, within the whole gardens and estate, but here in the Wildife Hide you have an opportunity to heighten your awareness. Although originally built as an observation point and a hub for pioneering technology – our emphasis now is more on offering information to enhance your whole visit and encouraging wildlife friendly activity both on and off site. Technology has moved on again since the heady days of 2007, when Hannibal the Heligan Barn Owlet featured on BBC *Springwatch*. Access to intimate wildlife footage is now relatively commonplace, so we want to invest in more hands-on education. This will include running a regular Wildlife Club for children and inviting visitor participation in a photography exhibition.

Barn Owls remain our Heligan icon and still live and breed on site. You can learn plenty about them as well as enjoying other wildlife footage recorded here at Heligan, highlighting the varied habitats that we manage across the whole site.

Our plan is to provide additional hides around the site for silent observation, retaining this building as a focus for information and encouragement across all ages and abilities. We have commissioned a collection of handmade wooden bird carvings, offering a tactile opportunity for identification – and each associated with its own acoustic birdcall. We want to help you appreciate not just the sights, but also the sounds and scents of the countryside - some of the secondary clues that bear witness to the wealth of wildlife here.

Great Spotted Woodpecker
(Dendrocopos major)

Managed Habitats

The simplest example of this is the microcosm of the whole estate presented immediately outside our Wildlife Hide. It in- cludes a pond, wild shrubbery, mature woodland and birdseed crop, all as a backdrop to daily feeding, specifically to attract and support particular species around the year.

The wider Heligan landscape offers predominantly pastures and woodland; but these are managed in various ways to present diverse habitats for wildlife. In the summer you may spot a variety of beautiful insects in Gillysame (the adjacent hay meadow), frogs, toads and dragonflies around the water courses in the valleys below. We grow swathes of cornfield annual flowers in various locations specifically to provide food as nectar for insects and later, seeds for birds. Otters, badgers and foxes are occasionally spotted and kingfishers and woodpeckers are evident in winter.

A rare Green Heron (Butorides virescens) *visited Heligan October 2010, from U.S.A.*

Cornfield annual wild flowers on East Lawn

TOUR 4 - *Explore*
Routes marked on map inside front cover

Woodland Sculptures

From the Ticket Office, proceed south, along Woodland Walk. This is the territory of the old shelterbelts for the gardens, planted by Henry Hawkins Tremayne two centuries ago; with increasingly regular gale- and storm-force winds, much new planting now helps to sustain this critical protection from the predominant south-westerlies. Swathes of Cornish daffodils bloom in March.

Immediately, the first woodland sculpture (created from an enormous upturned tree root after the Great Storm of 1990) entices you over. The Giant's Head was conceived and constructed by local artists, Sue Hill and her brother Pete, and has already inspired a generation, across the world. His hair of wild crocosmia turns orange during the summer, his green skin is 'Mind-your-own-business' and his eyes are made from broken blue china found in the estate's old bottle-dump *(below)*.

A few minutes later, further along Woodland Walk, you will come upon the Mud Maid, created by the same artists in the late 1990s, and now fast asleep under the trees. At certain times of year this is a particularly serene scene; when the spring light shafts down onto pools of bluebells or the snow lies like a blanket on the fields beyond. Quite magical... As you proceed along the path you may hear the sound of the woodpecker, tapping on dead wood above you.

A beautiful view soon opens up, with Grey Lady, Sue and Pete's third (and contrastingly insubstantial) woodland sculpture, standing sentinel at the top of Georgian Ride. 'Grey Lady's Walk' intersects from the left, where reputedly a shadowy figure was oft seen passing through, and away from Heligan House.

Foxgloves along Woodland Walk

Mud Maid in the snow

Grey Lady woodland sculpture by Sue Hill & Pete Hill. Photo © Scott Morrish/Glebe Cottage

West Lawn & Georgian Ride

Flanders Poppies (Papaver rhoeas) *create a sea of red on West Lawn during June/July*

Before you lies West Lawn, a large sloping field with an appealing view of Mevagissey in the distance. In recent years this ground has been dedicated to securing an expansive display of cornfield annual wildflowers, in order to attract a variety of insects in summer and, later, birds. The waves of colour can literally hum.

In spring 2014, as part of our commemoration of World War 1, we re-cultivated the ground using heavy horses and the Heligan team broad-cast by hand thousands of Flanders poppy seeds mixed with sand. These were to make an awesome impact the following year - and we intend to manage this Remembrance feature here over the remaining period of the Centenary.

At the bottom of the gravel path winding down across West Lawn, you will arrive at the top of The Jungle.

This fabulous exotic garden is described at the end of this section, from page 66. There is a map of The Jungle inside the back cover of this booklet.

Back at the top of West Lawn, the end of Woodland Walk is intersected by an historic route that used to run all the way from Heligan House on a circuit the width of a carriage, down into the valley and back up on the eastern side of the estate. You have the option of following this Georgian Ride by taking the turning right immediately beside Grey Lady. Thus you head south within continuing woodland shelter, skirting at a short distance the two fields to your left. Look out for our Bee Observation Hive on your left. (There is an opportunity to enter the second field, Valentines, through a farm gateway, and skirt the field down onto Butler's Path above The Jungle.) Frequently the Heligan Pigs are used to clear bramble here, ensuring that the spring wildflowers along Georgian Ride continue to create an exquisite kaleidoscope of colour, year on year. In Valentines, we focus more on summer cornfield annuals, attracting insects and birds with their nectar, pollen and seed.

If you choose to stay on Georgian Ride, the old track starts to descend quite steeply into the lower estate and as it swings around to the left, you may spot some new paths lined with short posts that lead up to another new installation.

Insect Hotel

An inspired development, requiring no permissions and constructed of wholly recycled materials! Everything from dried plant stems, dead leaves and rotting wood to clay bricks and old hedge stones is contrived to attract and support a breadth of wildlife. Continue on through an awesome landscape, crafted naturally and then hewn by man. Eventually Georgian Ride sweeps round to your left and you arrive in Lost Valley.

Insect Hotel on Georgian Ride/West

Lost Valley

This area, like the gardens, was discovered in a state of extreme neglect in the early 1990s. The name is not original; it echoes more recent history. The 1907 OS Map (*inside the front cover*) marks Heligan Mill to the south of Georgian Ride, where watercourses join forces from the west and from the north and flow east towards Mevagissey. It is the northern millstream that lies at the heart of Lost Valley today (running through Old Wood), while the Flour Mill is no longer in operation and lies downstream beyond our boundaries.

The old Georgian Ride continues its circuit right up through Lost Valley, lined by some extraordinary old oaks and beautiful mature beeches as well as conifers. Once you reach the charcoal sculpture and then the lakes, various paths intersect from the left as you proceed... Diagonal Path, Bottledump Hill and finally Sunken Lane – all steep, historic routes that served the back of Heligan House. Today, these will all set you on a homebound course towards the Steward's House, via East Lawn or Parc an Lann. Alternatively, you can stay in the valley and follow Georgian Ride in an almost complete loop, back up towards Gillysame and the Wildlife Hide.

Lost Valley is a haven for wildlife, with the lakes and watercourses attracting moorhen, frogs, toads and newts, bats and badgers, dragonflies, kingfishers and even otters. Settle quietly and take in the scene - ever changing by season.

Lost Valley is also a focus for traditional woodland practices, with coppicing and charcoal burning *(below)* still undertaken regularly. Mature sweet chestnuts evidence past practice – a living testament to century-old rural crafts. Our intention is to reintroduce more of these over the years ahead. Chiefly willow, hazel and sycamore are coppiced now, either for use in the gardens as pea or bean sticks or for charcoal burning. A large number of old charcoal burning platforms have been identified by archaeologists and our own sites are transient too. Resulting product today is high quality barbeque charcoal, which is sold from our Heligan Shop.

Georgian Ride into Lost Valley

The Lake in Lost Valley

Further Afield

Not for the faint-hearted, a detour up into the fields overlooking Lost Valley from the eastern boundary of The Estate will bring ample reward. Cross the valley on a narrow path between the two lakes and take the long, steep Tregassick Steps to your right, up the edge of Yonder Lantavy, an unimproved pasture used over many centuries. Here, we found a Cartwheel Penny dating back to the 1790s, possibly dropped by Thomas Gray while constructing his plans for Henry Hawkins's *ferme ornée* – the lay-out that we enjoy today. The view from the top of this field, out across the whole of his territory is exhilarating... the fine specimen trees of the valley, the awesome rhododendrons of The Gardens – and even a one-off glimpse of Heligan House, high up on the opposite bank, nestling within the foliage... exceptional location!

Walk all the way along the top of the field, inside the fence, until you join a very steep track running down to the left. This is Eastern Drive, possibly the oldest route in the whole estate, used by horses and carts for centuries. It connected Heligan to Mevagissey and the world beyond. The primroses here are a sight to behold in spring. Proceed down carefully until you join Georgian Ride once more and return home, most directly via Sunken Lane, to the Steward's House.

Alternatively you can continue all the way up the valley, close to the stream; either beside the pastures on the right-hand-side of the stream or along the remainder of Georgian Ride, until it swings round up to the left into the bottom of Gillysame. A steep climb will return you to the Wildlife Hide and Steward's House Café.

Autumn view north from Yonder Lantavy, across the old woodland of Lost Valley to the high, outer pastures of Heligan

THE JUNGLE
See inside back cover for Plan of Jungle Routes and Plantings

HELIGAN. FROM ORCHARD.

The Jungle (as it was named by locals after neglect since World War 1) is sited a short distance below Heligan House, in a very steep-sided valley which falls away in a south-easterly direction towards Mevagissey. You arrive at Top Pond via East or West Lawns for the classic vista *(opposite)* although you can also approach from its lower end in Lost Valley *(see map inside back flap)* or via Butler's Path. This exotic garden is sheltered from wind in all directions and harbours its own micro-climate, often remaining several degrees warmer than The Gardens – except in winter, when the frost can settle at its lowest point. Tender plantings can suffer badly in a hard freeze and several new collections have taken hits in recent years. However, the capacity for regeneration in these conditions is enormous!

The Jungle covers an area of eight acres, with a watercourse descending along the floor of the valley and linking four small ponds. It houses an historic collection of magnificent rhododendrons, conifers, palms, bamboos and other architectural plants from around the world, mostly sourced and planted by the last resident squire, Jack Tremayne.

Top Pond in The Jungle appears on the oldest known detailed map of Heligan, based on a survey done by William Hole in 1774. A footpath approached from the west, with a substantial orchard lying to the east. Subsequently Thomas Gray, who was employed by Henry Hawkins Tremayne to re-landscape the estate, proposed opening up the view of this area from the house. The St. Ewe Tithe Map of 1839 simply defines the

In the very early twentieth century Heligan House enjoyed a fine view down to Top Pond in the valley below. The scene has changed little in 100 years, except the fine herbaceous borders (opposite) *have been grassed over and creeper on the house cleared.*

Top Pond in spring

territory as 'Lawn' and 'Trees'. Henry's son, John Hearle Tremayne, who had a passion for trees, would have had access to the newly imported conifers arriving from the Americas during the 1840s and photos from around 1900 already show significant plantings on the banks.

The next historic map available is the 1881 Ordnance Survey. This shows the present Jungle area defined and a Second Pond lower down the valley, with watercourse marked. At this point the emerging garden was still known as 'The Orchard'. Butler's Path runs along the high western edge, linking Heligan House with Butler's Cottage down near the Mill and overlooking the length of the valley. There were already several intersecting routes which penetrated 'the interior'. The 1907 OS map shows a similar layout. We know that much of the rainwater run-off from The Gardens above was directed in pipes under Heligan House itself and feeds down into this valley. Successful management of rainwater and exploitation of natural watercourses are the fundamental to the development of many memorable gardens.

Jack Tremayne is largely responsible for the original exotic plant palette here, for during his lifetime (1869-1949) there was a phenomenal acceleration of plant imports from all around the world – and this became his passionate interest. The vistas opened up once more today demonstrate his flair and artistry in analysing the landscape and enhancing the topography with architectural specimens. Photographs from before World War 1 capture guests already belittled within this lost world. By the time Jack departed Heligan in 1923, this garden must have been spectacular.

Photo courtesy of Trudi Pitts

HYCAN FROM THE ORCHARD

One single recently discovered archival photo suggests that our rasied boardwalk is not a new idea!

However by 1990 this stunning garden had been completely choked by self-set sycamore and brambles and was cleared by the British Trust for Conservation Volunteers in working holidays over several years. It was decided to construct a raised boardwalk right down through the valley to protect the historic plantstock and create partial visitor access.

Our now historic plant collection originates from the Americas, Asia and Australasia. It includes a wide variety of conifers, notably a stand of monkey puzzles (*Araucaria araucana*), several large sequoias and an enormous *Podocarpus totara* beside Second Pond. There are long avenues of very tall Chusan palms (*Trachycarpus fortunei*), plantations of different bamboos and a string of ancient tree ferns (*Dicksonia antarctica*) along the floor of the valley. Original plantings of giant rhubarb (*Gunnera manicata*) and skunk cabbage (*Lysichiton americanus*) thrive in the bogs of the lower valley too. A significant backdrop of evergreen is provided by the extensive collection of old rhododendrons, including some stunning original Cornish Reds in an over-mature state *(opposite)*. All these dramatic plantings are a product of Jack's dynamic approach to plant acquisition and now provide the horticultural framework for this garden. Their conservation is our priority. Some specimens would have been purchased from Victorian nurseries only shortly after the plants were introduced to the UK; hence our inherited collection reflects the adventures of several great plant hunters.

Today's working methods are still determined by the dramatic topography of the site, with a lack of access both for vehicles and substantial machinery into the Jungle interior. This provides a considerable challenge for the team, who carry out most operations using only hand tools, wheelbarrows and waders. There are positive consequences from this approach, in that the whole environment is constantly peaceful and generally neither terrain nor ground flora suffers heavy physical damage. There is a regular schedule of work around the year, involving mulching, weeding, pruning, clearing, path and pond maintenance, as well as a constant eye on our veteran specimens and regular additions to planting. Monitoring and management of Sudden Oak Death is an ongoing issue.

Our new plantation of bananas, cannas and ginger lilies reaches its peak every autumn

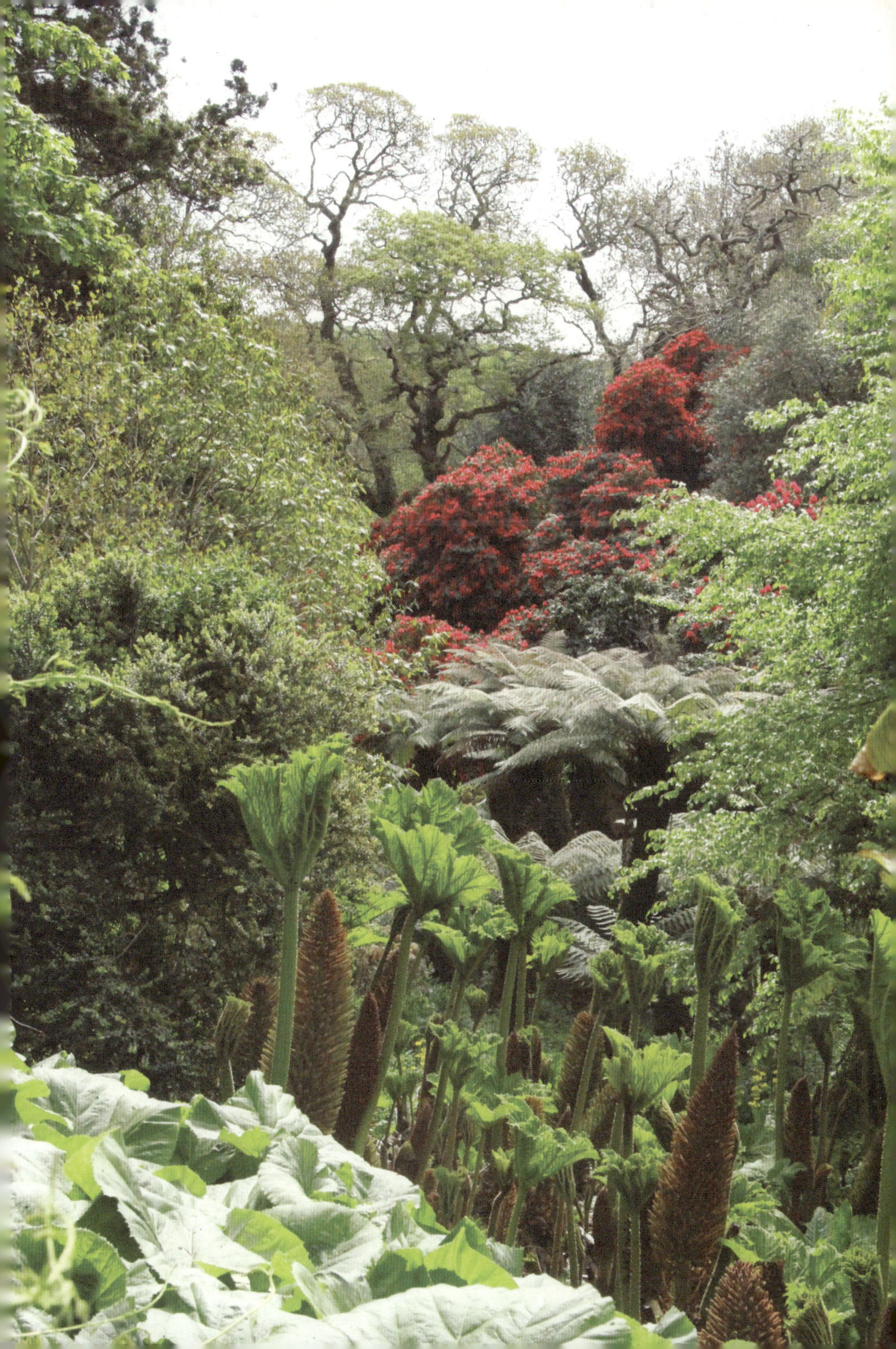

Tree ferns and ligularia down Fern Gulley

New Burma rope bridge - an aerial walk way above century - old tree ferns

Second Pond. Now and then.

Our own ethos of restoration within The Jungle reflects Jack's pioneering approach to plant acquisition, using the favourable micro-climate to trial subjects from around the world that may be new or unusual in the UK – or now rare, even in their original habitats. This contrasts with the ethos of period-correctness more strictly applied within The Gardens.

Most new planting projects have occurred on East Flank, where the slopes face the afternoon sun. These have included creating an outdoor protea and restio bed overlooking Top Pond and investment in stunning exotics like puya and echium, as well as a range of palms and a small grove of olives. Deeper into the valley we have established a substantial banana plantation interplanted with canna and ginger lilies and we are experimenting with exotic climbers and epiphytic plants. Along the boardwalk, unusual plants are being trialled to increase year-round interest.

Native flora and some remaining majestic oaks provide a beautiful compliment and contrast to all of the above and we encourage the snowdrops, primroses, wild garlic and bluebells, campion and foxgloves – while trying to control the more pernicious weeds.

Increasingly, as desirable plant cover takes a hold, the team is able to undertake more substantial new structural projects too. Recently this has included the creation of Gardeners' Walk in the far north-eastern corner, where a new conservation collection of Wollemi Pines from Australia is doing well amid ferns and bluebells.

Several new routes across the valley floor have been constructed to provide rich experiences during the months of frenetic summer growth. Fern Gulley links east and west boardwalks on the northern edge of Second Pond. A set of steps winds around a group of beautiful old tree ferns – tempting visitors down to the water's edge and crossing the stream beside a new marker stone for the Queen's Diamond Jubilee. On the south bank of Second Pond, you can rest awhile and watch the moorhen and dragonflies. At Third Pond, once again stroll down from the west to the water's edge, amid bananas (*Musa basjoo*) and giant rhubarb.

Finally, as you descend towards the bottom of the valley, a new Burma Rope Bridge is strung above the stream, as it courses through more almost primaeval-looking tree ferns and a host of bog plants and tropical climbers.

Cardiocrinum Lily

The impact of the whole is that The Jungle gives the appearance and indeed sometimes the experience of a far-away land lost in time (with barely a single distant pylon to break the spell). The drama of all the exotic plantings is a striking counterpoint to the massive native trees and delicate wild flora and fauna that also thrive in these conditions. The Jungle is frequented by a stunning array of wildlife – with the ever-present robin almost a Heligan mascot here. The valley attracts owls, otters, the odd kingfisher, various ducks and amphibians, beautiful dragonflies and even foxes into its secluded haven. The peaceful atmosphere creates sometimes almost heavenly experiences, with only the sound of the stream and the call of the birds to break the silence.

Trachycarpus fortunei in the lower Jungle

HELIGAN KITCHEN

Home-made Refreshments:

Fresh bread, scones, Cornish treats & cakes from our Bakery.

Morning breakfast, full seasonal meals and light snacks. Home-made soups, salads and sandwiches.

We source as many ingredients as we can from our own Productive Gardens:

Fresh Fruits, Vegetables, Salads, Flowers and Herbs.

and some from The Heligan Estate:

Home-reared Pork, Lamb & Beef, orchard fruits and wild herbs.

A selection of hot & cold drinks:

Fine Teas and Coffees, indulgent Hot Chocolate; locally produced juices, wines & beers...

And Finally!

Locally sourced Cornish pasties and delicious Cornish ice-cream.

A reduced selection from the above is available at the Steward's House Café, April-October, where there is also a garden for picknicking - for garden visitors only.

Photos © Albert Savage

HELIGAN SHOP & PLANT SALES

DIRECT FROM OUR WOODLANDS AND PRODUCED IN OUR KILNS:

Heligan Barbeque Charcoal.

DIRECT FROM OUR WORKSHOP:

A variety of items made from Heligan Wood.

HELIGAN HEAD GARDENER'S CHOICE

selections of Vegetable, Flower, Herb, Wild and Exotic Seeds.

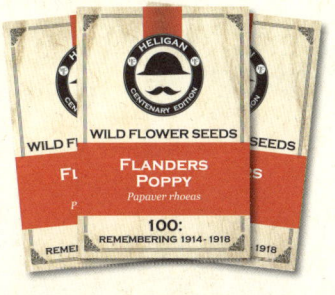

TRADITIONAL GARDEN TOOLS & EQUIPMENT AS RECOMMENDED BY OUR STAFF

A selection of fine quality locally produced plants & bulbs, reflecting the collections on display in The Gardens.

EXCLUSIVE PRODUCTS MADE BY PEOPLE WHO LOVE HELIGAN

including bread, ales, spirits, chocolate & preserves, china, bags, soaps, jewellery, books & cards.

HELIGAN LIBRARY

THE LOST GARDENS OF HELIGAN by Tim Smit
Updated by the author to the present day to celebrate 25 years since opening to the public and with a view to the future, this new full colour publication will include archival and contemporary photos and is expected to be available exclusively from Heligan in autumn 2017, pub. Orion. *Watch for news on our website later in the year.*

THE LOST GARDENS OF HELIGAN by Tim Smit. This gripping, award-winning tale recounts the many adventures of the early garden restoration. First published by Victor Gollancz in 1997, it is currently available as an Indigo paperback, pub. Orion; 2000. It includes four sections of full colour illustrations... a must read! **Price £10.99**

LOST GARDENS OF HELIGAN by Tim Smit. A German translation of the full original story, recently updated by the author and presented afresh in full colour with some new illustrations. 288 pages, pub. Ulmer; 2016. **Hardback £29.95**

HELIGAN SURVIVORS: *An Introduction to some of the Historic Plantstock discovered in the Lost Gardens of Heligan* inspired and edited by Philip McMillan Browse, pub. Alison Hodge; 2007.

A full-colour A4 paperback researched and written by Heligan staff, featuring the stories of 28 iconic Heligan plants, set against the history of their time. **Price £5**

THE LOST GARDENS OF HELIGAN: Camellias and Rhododendrons - National Plant Heritage Collection by Bee Robson, pub. Barman; 2010. Richly illustrated paperback summarising extensive research and pioneering development. **Price £9.95**

HELIGAN: FRUIT, FLOWERS AND HERBS by Philip McMillan Browse, pub. Alison Hodge; 2005. A beautiful full colour book, providing a comprehensive resource describing heritage crops grown at Heligan. **Price £10**

HELIGAN HISTORY CENTENARY EDITION: *Remembering Lost Men* by Candy Smit, pub. Heligan Gardens Ltd; 2014. This full colour 80-page booklet draws together all our research into past Heligan staff who not only gave service here to the Tremayne Family but also to King and Country during World War 1.

Richly illustrated with general and specific archival material, it details vividly descriptions of individual experiences. **Price £3.95**

HELIGAN: A CELEBRATION by Sue Lewington, pub. Truran; 2001. Favourite Heligan scenes feature in a delightful watercolour sketch book. **Paperback £4.99**

HELIGAN HARVEST by Sue Lewington, pub. Truran; 2003. The productive gardener's year is beautifully illustrated with evocative watercolour sketches and handwritten notes by the acclaimed Scillonian artist, informed by Heligan staff. Full colour. 136 pages. **Paperback £6.99**

HELIGAN DAYS: a perpetual diary illustrated by acclaimed local botanical artist, Mally Francis, with beautiful paintings of iconic Heligan plants and produce. Pub. Alison Hodge; 2006. **Hardback £7.99**

THE MUD MAID and **THE GIANT** — Two fabulous Heligan books for young children written by Sandra Horn and illustrated by Karen Popham, pub. The Clucket Press 2005 & 2006. **Paperbacks £5.99 each**

A CHILD'S KEEPSAKE OF HELIGAN — Photographic Heligan picture book for young children, featuring seasons, plants, tractors, food, animals, wildlife & mud sculptures. Fotogenix Publishing 2008. **Paperback £5**

A SONG FOR WILL by Hilary Robinson, illustrated by Martin Impey.
Without doubt a new children's classic from award-winning publishers, Strauss House Productions – indeed an exquisite book for all generations, this story is inspired by Heligan's status as A Living Memorial and crafted to honour former staff at Heligan who served in World War 1. It depicts many familiar places in the gardens as well as locally and was inspired by the first hand memories of family relatives of those who left their names on the Thunderbox wall for posterity. Ages 7-100! 68 pages in full colour. **Hardback £13.99**

Visit www.heligan.com for news of further new items

All prices are correct at the time of going to print. To place an order, please send your list of items with a cheque, payable to Heligan Gardens Ltd., along with the delivery address. Alternatively please call us with your card details. Standard postage for one order is £3.95 to a UK address. Receipt of goods can normally be expected within 14 days.